Table of Contents

Chapter 1: Introduction to AI Hardware

Understanding AI Hardware

In the subchapter "Understanding AI Hardware," we delve into the intricate world of artificial intelligence processors and the essential components that make up these advanced systems. For those seeking a comprehensive guide to AI hardware, this section provides a detailed comparison of various neural network processor architectures, shedding light on their unique features and capabilities. By understanding the differences between these architectures, readers can make informed decisions when selecting the most suitable hardware for their AI projects.

Moreover, this subchapter offers an in-depth analysis of the hardware requirements for training AI models, highlighting the key factors that impact performance and efficiency. From processing power to memory bandwidth, each component plays a crucial role in accelerating the training process and optimizing model accuracy. By mastering these hardware requirements, readers can enhance the speed and accuracy of their AI models, leading to more effective outcomes in various applications such as image recognition and natural language processing.

Furthermore, this section provides a guide to optimizing AI hardware for specific use cases, offering insights into the strategies and techniques that can enhance performance and efficiency. Whether it's fine-tuning hardware configurations or leveraging specialized processors, readers will learn how to tailor their hardware setups to meet the unique demands of different AI applications. By optimizing AI hardware, individuals can achieve superior performance and efficiency, unlocking new possibilities in the field of artificial intelligence.

Additionally, this subchapter reviews the latest advancements in AI hardware technology, exploring the cutting-edge innovations that are shaping the future of computing. From novel processor architectures to breakthroughs in hardware design, readers will gain valuable insights into the evolving landscape of AI hardware. By staying informed about the latest developments, individuals can stay ahead of the curve and leverage the most advanced hardware solutions for their AI projects.

In conclusion, "Understanding AI Hardware" offers a comprehensive overview of the components and functions of neural network processors, shedding light on their critical role in powering artificial intelligence applications. By exploring the impact of AI hardware on the future of computing, readers can gain a deeper understanding of the transformative potential of these advanced systems. Whether building custom AI hardware solutions or navigating the challenges and limitations of current technology, this subchapter equips individuals with the knowledge and insights needed to excel in the dynamic field of AI hardware.

Importance of AI Hardware in Neural Network Processors

In the realm of artificial intelligence (AI), the importance of AI hardware in neural network processors cannot be overstated. Neural network processors are at the heart of many AI applications, enabling machines to learn from data and make decisions with human-like intelligence. Understanding the role of AI hardware in this process is crucial for anyone looking to delve into the world of AI technology.

Neural network processors come in various architectures, each designed to optimize performance for specific tasks. From convolutional neural networks for image recognition to recurrent neural networks for natural language processing, different hardware requirements are needed to train and deploy AI models effectively. By delving into the intricacies of these architectures, individuals can gain a comprehensive understanding of how AI hardware influences the capabilities of neural network processors.

Optimizing AI hardware for specific use cases is essential for maximizing performance and efficiency. Whether it be fine-tuning hardware configurations for image recognition or enhancing processing power for natural language processing, customizing AI hardware solutions can significantly impact the success of AI applications. By exploring the ways in which AI hardware can be tailored to meet specific requirements, individuals can unlock the full potential of neural network processors in various domains.

As the field of AI hardware continues to evolve, staying abreast of the latest advancements is crucial for those looking to push the boundaries of AI technology. From breakthroughs in chip design to innovations in memory architecture, keeping up with the latest trends in AI hardware can provide valuable insights into the future of computing. By staying informed about the cutting-edge developments in AI hardware technology, individuals can position themselves at the forefront of AI innovation.

In conclusion, the importance of AI hardware in neural network processors cannot be overlooked in the ever-expanding landscape of artificial intelligence. By delving into the nuances of AI hardware architectures, optimizing hardware solutions for specific use cases, and staying informed about the latest advancements in AI hardware technology, individuals can gain a comprehensive understanding of how AI hardware influences the future of computing. With a keen focus on building custom AI hardware solutions and addressing the challenges and limitations of current AI hardware, individuals can pave the way for groundbreaking advancements in AI technology.

Overview of the Book

In the subchapter "Overview of the Book," readers will find a comprehensive guide to AI hardware, specifically focusing on neural network processors and beyond. Whether you are new to the world of AI hardware or looking to deepen your understanding, this book is designed to provide you with all the information you need to become an expert in the field.

One of the key aspects covered in this book is a detailed comparison of different neural network processor architectures. By exploring the strengths and weaknesses of various designs, readers will gain a deeper understanding of how these processors work and how they can be optimized for specific use cases such as image recognition or natural language processing.

Additionally, this book delves into the hardware requirements for training AI models, offering an in-depth analysis of the components needed to support efficient and effective training processes. Readers will also find a guide to optimizing AI hardware for specific use cases, helping them tailor their hardware solutions to meet the unique demands of their projects.

Furthermore, the book reviews the latest advancements in AI hardware technology, providing readers with insights into the cutting-edge developments shaping the future of computing. By breaking down the components and functions of a neural network processor, readers will gain a clear understanding of how these processors are revolutionizing the field of artificial intelligence.

Finally, this book explores the challenges and limitations of current AI hardware, offering a comparison with traditional computer hardware to highlight the unique benefits and considerations of specialized AI hardware. Readers will also find a discussion on the environmental impact of AI hardware and potential sustainability measures, shedding light on the broader implications of AI technology on our planet.

Chapter 2: Neural Network Processor Architectures

Types of Neural Network Processor Architectures

When it comes to neural network processor architectures, there are several types that are commonly used in the world of artificial intelligence. Each type has its own strengths and weaknesses, making it important for individuals interested in AI hardware to understand the differences between them.

One of the most common types of neural network processor architectures is the feedforward neural network. This type of architecture is characterized by its simple structure, with data flowing in one direction from input to output. Feedforward neural networks are often used for tasks such as image recognition and natural language processing, where the input data can be easily mapped to a specific output.

Another type of neural network processor architecture is the recurrent neural network. Unlike feedforward networks, recurrent neural networks have connections that loop back on themselves, allowing them to capture temporal dependencies in the data. This makes recurrent neural networks well-suited for tasks such as speech recognition and time series prediction.

Convolutional neural networks, or CNNs, are another popular type of architecture that is commonly used for tasks such as image recognition. CNNs are characterized by their use of convolutional layers, which apply filters to input data in order to extract relevant features. This makes CNNs highly effective at capturing spatial patterns in data.

In addition to feedforward, recurrent, and convolutional neural network architectures, there are also more specialized architectures that have been developed for specific tasks. For example, transformer architectures have been designed specifically for natural language processing tasks, while graph neural networks are well-suited for tasks involving graph-structured data.

Overall, understanding the different types of neural network processor architectures is essential for anyone looking to work in the field of AI hardware. By knowing the strengths and weaknesses of each type, individuals can choose the architecture that is best suited to their specific needs and optimize their hardware for maximum performance.

Comparison of Different Architectures

In this subchapter, we will delve into the intricate world of AI hardware by comparing different architectures used in neural network processors. Understanding the nuances of these architectures is crucial for anyone looking to master AI hardware and optimize its performance for specific use cases such as image recognition or natural language processing.

One of the key aspects we will explore is the hardware requirements for training AI models. By analyzing the components and functions of neural network processors, we can identify the optimal configurations needed to achieve efficient training and deployment of AI models. This in-depth analysis will provide valuable insights into building custom AI hardware solutions for research or industry applications.

Furthermore, we will discuss the latest advancements in AI hardware technology and their impact on the future of computing. By comparing traditional computer hardware with specialized AI hardware, we can gain a deeper understanding of the unique capabilities and limitations of each. This comparison will shed light on the challenges faced in developing AI hardware and potential sustainability measures to mitigate its environmental impact.

Through this comprehensive guide, we aim to equip you with the knowledge and tools necessary to navigate the complex landscape of AI hardware. Whether you are a researcher, developer, or industry professional, this subchapter will provide valuable insights into optimizing AI hardware for various applications and understanding its role in shaping the future of technology.

Pros and Cons of Each Architecture

In the world of AI hardware, there are various architectures to consider when designing neural network processors and other advanced technologies. Each architecture comes with its own set of pros and cons that can significantly impact the performance and efficiency of AI hardware systems. Understanding these differences is crucial for anyone looking to master AI hardware and optimize their systems for specific use cases.

One of the most common architectures used in AI hardware is the deep learning neural network processor. This architecture is known for its ability to handle complex computations and large datasets with high efficiency. The pros of this architecture include its scalability, parallel processing capabilities, and ability to perform well with deep learning algorithms. However, one of the cons of this architecture is its high power consumption, which can limit its practical applications in certain scenarios.

Another architecture to consider is the spiking neural network processor. This architecture is inspired by the way the human brain processes information, using spikes or pulses of activity to communicate between neurons. The pros of this architecture include its ability to mimic biological neural networks, leading to potentially more efficient and flexible AI systems. However, one of the cons of this architecture is its complexity and the challenges associated with programming and training spiking neural networks.

When it comes to hardware requirements for training AI models, different architectures have varying needs in terms of computational power, memory, and bandwidth. Understanding these requirements is essential for optimizing AI hardware for specific use cases, such as image recognition or natural language processing. By tailoring hardware configurations to the specific needs of a given AI model, users can achieve better performance and efficiency in their systems.

As advancements in AI hardware continue to push the boundaries of what is possible, it is important to stay informed about the latest technologies and trends in the field. Keeping up with the latest advancements can help users make more informed decisions about their hardware choices and stay ahead of the curve in a rapidly evolving industry. By staying informed and continuously learning about the latest advancements in AI hardware technology, individuals can position themselves as leaders in the field and drive innovation in the future of computing.

In conclusion, understanding the pros and cons of different AI hardware architectures is essential for anyone looking to master the field. By comparing and analyzing the various architectures available, individuals can make more informed decisions about their hardware choices and optimize their systems for specific use cases. With a comprehensive understanding of the hardware requirements, advancements, challenges, and environmental impact of AI hardware, individuals can build custom solutions that push the boundaries of what is possible in AI technology.

Chapter 3: Hardware Requirements for Training AI Models

Processing Power and Memory Requirements

In the world of artificial intelligence, processing power and memory requirements play a crucial role in the efficiency and effectiveness of neural network processors. Understanding these factors is essential for anyone looking to delve deep into the realm of AI hardware. In this subchapter, we will explore the intricate details of processing power and memory requirements, shedding light on how they impact the performance of neural network processors.

When it comes to processing power, neural network processors are designed to handle complex mathematical computations at high speeds. The ability to process vast amounts of data quickly is essential for training and running AI models efficiently. Different neural network processor architectures offer varying levels of processing power, with some focusing on parallel processing to accelerate computations. Understanding the nuances of these architectures is key to selecting the right hardware for your specific AI applications.

Memory requirements also play a significant role in the performance of neural network processors. AI models often require large amounts of memory to store data, weights, and intermediate results during training and inference. The type and capacity of memory integrated into neural network processors can greatly impact their performance. Balancing processing power and memory capacity is crucial for optimizing AI hardware for tasks such as image recognition or natural language processing.

As advancements in AI hardware technology continue to push the boundaries of what is possible, it is essential to stay informed about the latest developments in processing power and memory requirements. Building custom AI hardware solutions for research or industry applications requires a deep understanding of these factors to ensure optimal performance. By staying up-to-date on the latest advancements in AI hardware technology, you can leverage the power of neural network processors to drive innovation in the field of artificial intelligence.

In conclusion, processing power and memory requirements are fundamental aspects of AI hardware that have a profound impact on the efficiency and performance of neural network processors. By understanding the intricacies of these factors and staying informed about the latest advancements in AI hardware technology, you can harness the full potential of neural network processors for a wide range of applications. Whether you are a researcher, developer, or industry professional, mastering the complexities of processing power and memory requirements is essential for unlocking the true power of artificial intelligence.

Data Storage and Bandwidth Considerations

In the world of artificial intelligence (AI), data storage and bandwidth considerations play a crucial role in the performance and efficiency of neural network processors. Understanding these factors is essential for anyone looking to delve into the realm of AI hardware. This subchapter will provide a comprehensive guide to help you navigate through the intricacies of data storage and bandwidth considerations in AI hardware.

When it comes to data storage, neural network processors rely heavily on high-speed memory to store and access vast amounts of data efficiently. The type of memory used, such as SRAM or DRAM, can significantly impact the performance of AI models. Additionally, the size of the memory and its access latency are crucial factors to consider when designing AI hardware for optimal performance.

Bandwidth considerations are equally important in AI hardware, as the speed at which data can be transferred between different components directly affects the overall efficiency of neural network processors. High bandwidth ensures that data can flow seamlessly between memory, processing units, and other components, allowing for faster computation and improved performance. It is essential to carefully design the interconnects and communication pathways within AI hardware to maximize bandwidth and minimize latency.

Optimizing AI hardware for specific use cases, such as image recognition or natural language processing, requires a deep understanding of data storage and bandwidth considerations. By tailoring the hardware architecture to the specific requirements of the AI model being trained, developers can achieve significant performance gains and efficiency improvements. This subchapter will explore different strategies for optimizing AI hardware for various applications, providing valuable insights for those looking to enhance their AI hardware designs.

As technology continues to advance, the field of AI hardware is constantly evolving. Keeping up with the latest advancements in data storage and bandwidth technologies is essential for staying ahead of the curve. This subchapter will provide a review of the latest developments in AI hardware technology, including new memory technologies, interconnect designs, and bandwidth optimization techniques. By staying informed on the latest trends in AI hardware, you can ensure that your designs are always at the cutting edge of innovation.

In conclusion, data storage and bandwidth considerations are fundamental aspects of AI hardware design that can greatly impact the performance and efficiency of neural network processors. By understanding the intricacies of these factors and optimizing hardware designs accordingly, developers can unlock the full potential of AI models and achieve groundbreaking results. This subchapter aims to provide a comprehensive guide to help you navigate the complexities of data storage and bandwidth considerations in AI hardware, empowering you to create innovative solutions for a wide range of applications.

Optimization Techniques for Training

Optimization techniques for training play a crucial role in maximizing the performance of AI hardware, particularly neural network processors. In this subchapter, we will delve into various strategies and methods that can be employed to enhance the efficiency and effectiveness of training AI models. These techniques are essential for achieving faster training times, improved accuracy, and reduced energy consumption, ultimately leading to more powerful and cost-effective AI solutions.

One key optimization technique for training AI models is parallel processing, which involves breaking down the training data into smaller batches and processing them simultaneously on multiple cores or processors. This allows for faster computations and can significantly accelerate the training process. Additionally, techniques such as data augmentation, regularization, and dropout can be used to prevent overfitting and improve the generalization capabilities of the model.

Another important aspect of optimizing AI hardware for training is the selection of appropriate hyperparameters, such as learning rate, batch size, and network architecture. Fine-tuning these parameters can have a significant impact on the performance of the model and can help achieve better accuracy and convergence speed. Furthermore, techniques such as transfer learning and model compression can be utilized to reduce the computational complexity of the model and improve its efficiency.

In addition to optimizing the training process itself, it is also essential to consider hardware-specific optimizations that can further enhance the performance of AI models. This includes utilizing specialized hardware accelerators, such as GPUs, TPUs, or FPGAs, which are designed to perform matrix multiplication and other computations required for training neural networks more efficiently. Additionally, techniques such as quantization, sparsity, and model pruning can be used to reduce the memory and computational requirements of the model, leading to faster inference and lower energy consumption.

Overall, the optimization techniques discussed in this subchapter are crucial for maximizing the performance of AI hardware for training purposes. By implementing these strategies and methods, researchers and practitioners can achieve faster training times, improved accuracy, and reduced energy consumption, ultimately leading to more powerful and cost-effective AI solutions.

Chapter 4: Optimizing AI Hardware for Specific Use Cases

Image Recognition Applications

Image recognition applications are one of the most widely used and exciting uses of AI hardware in today's technological landscape. From facial recognition on smartphones to autonomous vehicles identifying objects on the road, image recognition has become an integral part of our daily lives. In this subchapter, we will delve into the various applications of image recognition and how AI hardware plays a crucial role in making these tasks possible.

One of the key applications of image recognition is in the field of healthcare, where AI-powered systems can assist doctors in diagnosing diseases such as cancer or identifying anomalies in medical images. By utilizing neural network processors, these systems can quickly analyze large amounts of image data with high accuracy, leading to more efficient and accurate diagnoses.

In the realm of security and surveillance, image recognition technology is used to identify and track individuals in real-time, enhancing the capabilities of security systems in public spaces, airports, and other high-security areas. Neural network processors are essential for processing the vast amount of visual data captured by surveillance cameras and quickly identifying potential threats or suspects.

Image recognition also plays a crucial role in e-commerce, where AI-powered systems can recommend products to customers based on their browsing history and preferences. By analyzing images of products and matching them to similar items, these systems can provide personalized recommendations that enhance the shopping experience for consumers.

Furthermore, image recognition technology is being increasingly used in the automotive industry for applications such as autonomous driving and driver assistance systems. By using AI hardware to process images from cameras mounted on vehicles, these systems can detect road signs, pedestrians, and other vehicles, enabling safer and more efficient driving experiences.

Overall, image recognition applications are just one example of how AI hardware, such as neural network processors, is revolutionizing various industries and shaping the future of computing. By understanding the capabilities and limitations of AI hardware in image recognition tasks, individuals can harness the power of this technology to create innovative solutions that drive progress and improve efficiency in a wide range of applications.

Natural Language Processing Applications

Natural Language Processing (NLP) is a branch of artificial intelligence that focuses on the interaction between computers and human language. NLP applications have become increasingly popular in recent years, with advancements in AI hardware enabling more efficient and accurate processing of natural language. From virtual assistants like Siri and Alexa to language translation services and sentiment analysis tools, NLP is transforming the way we interact with technology on a daily basis.

One of the key challenges in NLP applications is the ability to process and understand human language in a way that is both accurate and efficient. This requires specialized hardware that is capable of handling the complex computations involved in natural language processing tasks. Neural network processors, with their parallel processing capabilities and ability to handle large amounts of data, have emerged as a key technology for powering NLP applications.

When it comes to optimizing AI hardware for NLP tasks, there are a number of factors to consider. These include the type of neural network architecture being used, the size of the dataset being processed, and the specific requirements of the NLP application in question. By carefully tuning the hardware to meet the unique demands of natural language processing, developers can achieve significant improvements in performance and accuracy.

In recent years, there have been significant advancements in AI hardware technology that have further enhanced the capabilities of NLP applications. From the development of specialized NLP processors to the integration of advanced algorithms and techniques, researchers and engineers are constantly pushing the boundaries of what is possible with natural language processing. These advancements are not only improving the accuracy and efficiency of NLP applications but also opening up new possibilities for how we interact with technology.

As we look to the future, it is clear that AI hardware will play a crucial role in shaping the development of NLP applications and other AI technologies. By understanding the unique requirements of natural language processing and optimizing hardware to meet these demands, developers can unlock new possibilities for how we communicate and interact with machines. With continued advancements in AI hardware technology, the potential for NLP applications to revolutionize industries and improve our daily lives is truly limitless.

Real-time Decision Making

Real-time decision making is a critical aspect of artificial intelligence (AI) hardware that allows for quick and efficient processing of data to make informed choices. In the realm of neural network processors and other AI hardware technologies, real-time decision making plays a vital role in improving performance and accuracy. This subchapter will delve into the intricacies of real-time decision making in AI hardware, providing a comprehensive guide for those looking to enhance their understanding of this essential concept.

When it comes to real-time decision making in AI hardware, speed is of the essence. Neural network processors are designed to process vast amounts of data quickly and efficiently, allowing for rapid decision-making capabilities. By utilizing specialized architectures and algorithms, AI hardware can analyze data in real-time, enabling faster responses to changing conditions and inputs. This speed is crucial in applications such as autonomous vehicles, where split-second decisions can mean the difference between safety and disaster.

In order to achieve real-time decision making in AI hardware, specific hardware requirements must be met. These include high-performance processors, efficient memory systems, and optimized algorithms for quick data processing. By understanding and implementing these requirements, developers can create AI hardware solutions that excel in real-time decision making, leading to improved performance and reliability in various applications.

Optimizing AI hardware for specific use cases, such as image recognition or natural language processing, is another crucial aspect of real-time decision making. By tailoring hardware designs to meet the demands of specific applications, developers can enhance performance and efficiency, ultimately leading to more accurate and timely decisions. This optimization process involves fine-tuning hardware components and algorithms to meet the unique requirements of each use case, ensuring that AI systems can make real-time decisions with precision and speed.

In conclusion, real-time decision making is a fundamental aspect of AI hardware that drives performance, efficiency, and reliability in various applications. By understanding the intricacies of real-time decision making and optimizing hardware designs for specific use cases, developers can create AI solutions that excel in processing data quickly and accurately. With advancements in neural network processors and other AI technologies, real-time decision making will continue to play a crucial role in shaping the future of computing and driving innovation in AI hardware.

Chapter 5: Latest Advancements in AI Hardware Technology

Introduction to Quantum Computing

In recent years, quantum computing has emerged as a revolutionary technology with the potential to transform the field of artificial intelligence. For those eager to delve into the world of AI hardware, understanding quantum computing is essential. This subchapter will provide a comprehensive introduction to quantum computing, exploring its fundamental principles and how it differs from classical computing.

Quantum computing leverages the principles of quantum mechanics to perform complex calculations at speeds unimaginable with traditional computers. Unlike classical bits, which can only exist in a state of 0 or 1, quantum bits, or qubits, can exist in a superposition of states, allowing for parallel processing and exponential computational power. This unique characteristic enables quantum computers to tackle problems that are currently intractable for classical computers, such as simulating chemical reactions, optimizing financial portfolios, and training complex AI models.

One of the most intriguing aspects of quantum computing is its potential to accelerate AI training and inference tasks. By harnessing the power of quantum superposition and entanglement, quantum computers can explore vast solution spaces in a fraction of the time it would take a classical computer. This has profound implications for the field of AI, as it could lead to breakthroughs in areas such as natural language processing, image recognition, and autonomous driving.

As we delve deeper into the realm of quantum computing, it is important to understand the hardware requirements for building and optimizing quantum processors. Quantum computers require specialized components, such as superconducting qubits, trapped ions, and topological qubits, each with its own advantages and challenges. Moreover, optimizing quantum hardware for specific AI tasks involves designing efficient quantum algorithms, minimizing error rates, and mitigating decoherence effects.

In the coming chapters, we will explore the latest advancements in quantum computing hardware, the impact of quantum technology on the future of AI, and the challenges and limitations that researchers and engineers face in developing scalable quantum processors. By mastering the principles of quantum computing, AI enthusiasts can unlock new possibilities for accelerating innovation and pushing the boundaries of artificial intelligence.

Neuromorphic Computing

Neuromorphic computing is a cutting-edge approach to AI hardware that mimics the structure and function of the human brain. This technology is revolutionizing the field of artificial intelligence by enabling machines to process information in a more efficient and intelligent manner. In this subchapter, we will delve into the intricacies of neuromorphic computing and explore its potential applications and impact on the future of computing.

One of the key features of neuromorphic computing is its ability to perform complex computations in a parallel and distributed manner, similar to the way neurons communicate in the brain. This allows for faster processing speeds and lower power consumption compared to traditional computing architectures. By leveraging this unique approach, neural network processors can handle large amounts of data and perform tasks such as image recognition and natural language processing with greater accuracy and efficiency.

In order to fully understand the capabilities of neuromorphic computing, it is important to compare and contrast different neural network processor architectures. Each architecture has its own strengths and weaknesses, and choosing the right one for a specific application is crucial for optimal performance. By examining the inner workings of these processors, we can gain a deeper understanding of how they function and how they can be optimized for specific use cases.

Training AI models requires significant computational power, and traditional hardware may not be able to keep up with the demands of complex neural networks. This is where specialized AI hardware, such as neuromorphic processors, comes into play. These processors are designed to efficiently train and execute AI models, enabling researchers and industry professionals to push the boundaries of what is possible in the field of artificial intelligence.

As we look towards the future of computing, it is clear that AI hardware will play a pivotal role in shaping the way we interact with technology. By building custom solutions tailored to specific applications and optimizing hardware for performance and efficiency, we can unlock new possibilities in areas such as healthcare, finance, and autonomous vehicles. The advancements in neuromorphic computing technology are paving the way for a new era of intelligent machines that can learn, adapt, and make decisions in ways that were previously unimaginable.

Edge Computing Solutions

In the realm of artificial intelligence, edge computing solutions have emerged as a pivotal component in the advancement of AI hardware technology. Edge computing refers to the practice of processing data closer to the source, reducing latency and enhancing efficiency in AI applications. In this subchapter, we will delve into the intricacies of edge computing solutions, providing a comprehensive guide for individuals seeking to understand the nuances of AI hardware.

One of the key aspects of edge computing solutions is the utilization of neural network processors, which are specifically designed to accelerate AI workloads. By comparing different neural network processor architectures, readers will gain a deeper insight into the various options available in the market. This detailed comparison will enable individuals to make informed decisions when selecting the most suitable hardware for their specific AI applications.

Furthermore, an in-depth analysis of hardware requirements for training AI models will be provided, offering readers a comprehensive understanding of the computational resources necessary for optimal performance. Additionally, a guide to optimizing AI hardware for specific use cases, such as image recognition or natural language processing, will be explored, showcasing the versatility and adaptability of AI hardware solutions.

As technology continues to evolve, it is crucial to stay abreast of the latest advancements in AI hardware technology. This subchapter will review the cutting-edge developments in the field, highlighting the innovative solutions that are shaping the future of computing. By breaking down the components and functions of a neural network processor, readers will gain a deeper appreciation for the underlying mechanisms driving AI hardware innovation.

Ultimately, the impact of AI hardware on the future of computing cannot be understated. As we navigate the complexities of building custom AI hardware solutions for research or industry applications, it is essential to consider the challenges and limitations that may arise. By comparing traditional computer hardware with specialized AI hardware, readers will gain valuable insights into the unique capabilities and constraints of each system, paving the way for informed decision-making in the ever-evolving landscape of AI hardware technology.

Chapter 6: Components and Functions of a Neural Network Processor

Processing Units

In the world of artificial intelligence, processing units play a vital role in the execution of complex neural networks. These units are specifically designed to handle the massive amounts of data and computations required for training and inference tasks. In this subchapter, we will delve into the intricacies of processing units, exploring their architecture, functions, and impact on the future of AI hardware.

There are various types of processing units used in AI hardware, each with its own unique characteristics and capabilities. From traditional CPUs and GPUs to specialized neural network processors, the choice of processing unit can significantly impact the performance and efficiency of AI models. In this guide, we will provide a detailed comparison of different neural network processor architectures, highlighting their strengths and weaknesses in various applications.

Training AI models requires significant computational power and memory bandwidth, making hardware requirements a critical consideration for researchers and developers. We will discuss the in-depth analysis of hardware requirements for training AI models, including the importance of factors such as parallelism, memory hierarchy, and power efficiency. By optimizing hardware configurations, users can enhance the performance of AI models and reduce training times.

Optimizing AI hardware for specific use cases, such as image recognition or natural language processing, requires a deep understanding of the underlying algorithms and computational requirements. We will provide a guide to optimizing AI hardware for different applications, exploring techniques such as quantization, pruning, and model parallelism. By tailoring hardware solutions to specific use cases, users can achieve improved performance and energy efficiency.

As the field of AI hardware continues to evolve, the latest advancements in technology are shaping the future of computing. We will review the latest trends in AI hardware technology, including advancements in neuromorphic computing, quantum computing, and silicon photonics. By staying informed about the latest developments, users can leverage cutting-edge hardware solutions to drive innovation in AI research and industry applications.

Memory Architecture

Memory architecture plays a crucial role in the performance and efficiency of AI hardware, especially neural network processors. In this subchapter, we will delve into the intricacies of memory architecture and its impact on training and inference tasks. Understanding memory architecture is essential for optimizing AI hardware for specific use cases, such as image recognition or natural language processing.

When it comes to neural network processors, memory architecture refers to how data is stored, accessed, and manipulated within the hardware. The choice of memory architecture can significantly affect the speed, power consumption, and overall performance of AI models. For example, a well-designed memory architecture can reduce the latency of data retrieval, leading to faster training and inference times.

Different neural network processor architectures have varying memory hierarchies, including on-chip caches, shared memory, and off-chip memory. Each type of memory has its own advantages and disadvantages, and the optimal memory architecture depends on the specific requirements of the AI model being used. By understanding the trade-offs between different memory architectures, developers can make informed decisions to maximize the performance of their AI hardware.

In order to train AI models effectively, it is important to consider the hardware requirements for memory bandwidth, capacity, and latency. Memory bandwidth determines the rate at which data can be transferred between the processor and memory, while memory capacity dictates the amount of data that can be stored at any given time. Additionally, memory latency refers to the time it takes for the processor to access data from memory, which can impact the overall performance of the AI model.

Overall, memory architecture plays a critical role in shaping the capabilities and limitations of AI hardware. By understanding the nuances of memory architecture, developers can optimize their hardware for specific use cases and enhance the performance of their AI models. Stay tuned as we explore the latest advancements in memory architecture and their implications for the future of AI hardware.

Interconnectivity

Interconnectivity plays a crucial role in the field of AI hardware, as it refers to the ability of different components within a system to communicate and share information effectively. In the context of neural network processors, interconnectivity is essential for enabling efficient data transfer between processing units, memory modules, and other hardware components. By optimizing the interconnectivity within a system, developers can enhance the overall performance and efficiency of AI hardware, leading to faster processing speeds and improved accuracy in AI models.

When comparing different neural network processor architectures, one of the key factors to consider is the level of interconnectivity between processing units. Some architectures may feature a centralized interconnect, where all processing units communicate through a single controller, while others may utilize a distributed interconnect, allowing for parallel communication between multiple processing units simultaneously. Understanding the trade-offs between these architectures can help developers choose the most suitable design for their specific AI applications.

In order to meet the hardware requirements for training AI models, it is essential to consider the interconnectivity between processing units and memory modules. High-bandwidth interconnects are crucial for enabling fast data transfer between processing units and memory, allowing for efficient training of large-scale neural networks. By optimizing the interconnectivity within a system, developers can reduce training times and improve the scalability of their AI models.

Optimizing AI hardware for specific use cases, such as image recognition or natural language processing, requires careful consideration of the interconnectivity between different components. For example, in image recognition tasks, efficient communication between processing units and memory modules is essential for processing large amounts of image data in real-time. By optimizing the interconnectivity within a system, developers can improve the performance and accuracy of their AI models for specific applications.

In conclusion, interconnectivity plays a critical role in the design and optimization of AI hardware, enabling efficient communication and data transfer between different components within a system. By understanding the impact of interconnectivity on neural network processor architectures, hardware requirements for training AI models, and optimization for specific use cases, developers can design more efficient and scalable AI hardware solutions. With the constant advancements in AI hardware technology, optimizing interconnectivity will continue to be a key focus for improving the performance and capabilities of AI systems in the future.

Chapter 7: Impact of AI Hardware on the Future of Computing

Integration with Traditional Computing Systems

Integration with traditional computing systems is a crucial aspect of mastering AI hardware. As AI technology continues to advance, the need to seamlessly integrate neural network processors and other specialized hardware with traditional computing systems becomes more apparent. This integration allows for the efficient processing of AI algorithms and the seamless transfer of data between different components of a computing system. Understanding how AI hardware can work in tandem with traditional computing systems is essential for achieving optimal performance and maximizing the capabilities of AI technology.

One of the key challenges in integrating AI hardware with traditional computing systems is ensuring compatibility and interoperability between different components. Traditional computing systems are typically designed to work with general-purpose processors and may not be optimized for the specialized requirements of AI algorithms. To address this challenge, developers must carefully design and implement interfaces that allow for the seamless communication between AI hardware and traditional computing systems. This may involve developing specialized drivers, APIs, and protocols to facilitate data transfer and processing between different components of a computing system.

Another important consideration when integrating AI hardware with traditional computing systems is the efficient utilization of resources. AI algorithms often require significant computational power and memory bandwidth to perform complex tasks such as image recognition or natural language processing. Traditional computing systems may not be equipped to handle the high demands of AI algorithms, leading to performance bottlenecks and inefficiencies. By optimizing the integration of AI hardware with traditional computing systems, developers can ensure that resources are efficiently utilized and that AI algorithms can run smoothly and efficiently.

In addition to optimizing resource utilization, integrating AI hardware with traditional computing systems also involves ensuring the security and reliability of the system. AI algorithms often deal with sensitive data and require high levels of security to protect against cyber threats and data breaches. By implementing robust security measures and protocols, developers can ensure that AI algorithms can run securely on traditional computing systems without compromising data integrity or system performance.

Overall, mastering the integration of AI hardware with traditional computing systems is essential for unlocking the full potential of AI technology. By understanding the challenges and considerations involved in integrating AI hardware with traditional computing systems, developers can optimize performance, resource utilization, security, and reliability to create powerful and efficient AI solutions. With the right approach and expertise, developers can harness the power of AI hardware to revolutionize computing systems and drive innovation in various industries.

Potential Applications in Various Industries

In the realm of AI hardware, the potential applications span across various industries, showcasing the versatility and transformative power of neural network processors and beyond. From healthcare to finance, transportation to entertainment, the impact of AI hardware is profound and far-reaching. This subchapter delves into the myriad possibilities and opportunities for leveraging AI hardware in different sectors, providing insights for those seeking to harness the full potential of this cutting-edge technology.

One of the key areas where AI hardware is making a significant impact is in healthcare. From diagnosing diseases to personalizing treatment plans, neural network processors are revolutionizing the way medical professionals approach patient care. By analyzing vast amounts of data and identifying patterns that might elude human clinicians, AI hardware is helping to improve outcomes and save lives. With the potential to enhance medical imaging, drug discovery, and genomics, the applications of AI hardware in healthcare are limitless.

In the realm of finance, AI hardware is driving innovation and efficiency, enabling institutions to make faster and more accurate decisions. From algorithmic trading to fraud detection, neural network processors are powering advanced analytics and predictive modeling, leading to better risk management and improved customer experiences. By leveraging AI hardware, financial institutions can gain a competitive edge and stay ahead of rapidly evolving market trends.

In the transportation sector, AI hardware is playing a crucial role in shaping the future of autonomous vehicles and smart transportation systems. By processing real-time data from sensors and cameras, neural network processors enable vehicles to navigate complex environments and make split-second decisions. With the potential to reduce accidents, improve traffic flow, and enhance passenger safety, AI hardware is paving the way for a new era of mobility.

In the entertainment industry, AI hardware is fueling creativity and innovation, enabling artists and creators to push the boundaries of what is possible. From generating realistic graphics to enhancing virtual reality experiences, neural network processors are powering immersive entertainment experiences that captivate audiences and redefine storytelling. With the potential to revolutionize content creation and distribution, AI hardware is reshaping the entertainment landscape and opening up new possibilities for immersive storytelling.

Ethical Considerations

Ethical considerations play a crucial role in the development and deployment of AI hardware, especially in the realm of neural network processors. As we delve deeper into the world of artificial intelligence, it is essential to address the ethical implications of using this technology. This subchapter will explore the ethical considerations that must be taken into account when designing, building, and utilizing AI hardware.

One of the primary ethical considerations in AI hardware is the issue of bias. Neural network processors are trained on vast amounts of data, which can sometimes contain biases that reflect societal prejudices. It is crucial to ensure that these biases are identified and mitigated to prevent discriminatory outcomes in AI applications. Ethical guidelines must be established to promote fairness and transparency in the development of neural network processors.

Another ethical consideration in AI hardware is privacy. As neural network processors become more sophisticated and capable of processing sensitive data, it is essential to protect the privacy of individuals. Data security measures must be implemented to safeguard personal information and prevent unauthorized access. Additionally, data anonymization techniques should be employed to ensure that user privacy is respected.

Furthermore, the ethical implications of AI hardware extend to issues of accountability and transparency. It is essential for developers and manufacturers of neural network processors to be transparent about how their technology functions and the potential risks associated with its use. Clear guidelines must be established to determine who is responsible in the event of AI errors or malfunctions, ensuring accountability in the deployment of AI hardware.

In conclusion, ethical considerations are paramount in the development and deployment of AI hardware, particularly neural network processors. By addressing issues of bias, privacy, accountability, and transparency, we can ensure that AI technology is used responsibly and ethically. It is essential for individuals and organizations involved in AI hardware to uphold ethical standards and prioritize the well-being of society as we continue to advance in this field.

Chapter 8: Building Custom AI Hardware Solutions

Research Applications

In the realm of artificial intelligence (AI) hardware, research applications play a crucial role in pushing the boundaries of what is possible with neural network processors and beyond. For a person that wants to learn everything there is to know about AI hardware, understanding the various research applications is essential for gaining a comprehensive understanding of the field.

One key aspect of research applications in AI hardware is the detailed comparison of different neural network processor architectures. By examining the strengths and weaknesses of various architectures, researchers can better understand how to optimize hardware for specific use cases, such as image recognition or natural language processing. This analysis helps guide the development of more efficient and powerful hardware solutions for AI tasks.

Another important aspect of research applications in AI hardware is the in-depth analysis of hardware requirements for training AI models. Understanding the computational demands of training neural networks is essential for designing hardware that can handle the massive amounts of data and complex calculations involved in AI model training. Researchers must consider factors such as memory bandwidth, processing power, and energy efficiency when designing hardware for AI training tasks.

Furthermore, research applications in AI hardware involve optimizing hardware for specific use cases. By tailoring hardware solutions to meet the unique requirements of tasks like image recognition or natural language processing, researchers can achieve higher levels of performance and efficiency. This optimization process may involve customizing hardware components, developing specialized algorithms, or utilizing advanced techniques such as parallel processing.

Overall, research applications in AI hardware encompass a wide range of topics, from the latest advancements in technology to the challenges and limitations facing the field. By exploring these research applications, individuals can gain a deeper understanding of how AI hardware is shaping the future of computing and driving innovation in industries ranging from healthcare to finance. Whether building custom hardware solutions for research or industry applications, researchers must stay informed about the latest developments and trends in AI hardware to stay ahead of the curve.

Industry Applications

In the realm of artificial intelligence, the applications of AI hardware are vast and ever-expanding. From neural network processors to specialized hardware for image recognition and natural language processing, the industry applications of AI hardware are crucial for advancing the field of AI. In this subchapter, we will delve into the various ways in which AI hardware is being utilized in different industries, providing a comprehensive guide for those eager to learn more about this cutting-edge technology.

One of the key aspects of AI hardware is its ability to optimize performance for specific use cases. Whether it be image recognition, natural language processing, or other AI tasks, hardware requirements play a crucial role in training AI models efficiently. Understanding the hardware specifications needed for different applications is essential for achieving optimal performance in AI tasks.

Furthermore, advancements in AI hardware technology are constantly pushing the boundaries of what is possible in the field of artificial intelligence. From improved neural network processor architectures to custom hardware solutions for research and industry applications, the landscape of AI hardware is evolving at a rapid pace. This subchapter will provide a detailed comparison of different neural network processor architectures, as well as a discussion on the impact of AI hardware on the future of computing.

As we explore the components and functions of a neural network processor, we will also address the challenges and limitations of current AI hardware. While AI hardware has the potential to revolutionize various industries, there are still hurdles to overcome in terms of scalability, power consumption, and environmental impact. By comparing traditional computer hardware with specialized AI hardware, we can gain a deeper understanding of the unique capabilities and limitations of each.

In conclusion, this subchapter on industry applications of AI hardware serves as a comprehensive guide for those looking to gain a thorough understanding of this revolutionary technology. From optimizing hardware for specific use cases to building custom solutions for research and industry applications, the potential of AI hardware is vast. By staying informed on the latest advancements in AI hardware technology, we can harness the power of artificial intelligence to drive innovation and progress in various industries.

Considerations for Design and Development

When it comes to designing and developing AI hardware, there are several key considerations that must be taken into account. From understanding the specific requirements of neural network processors to optimizing hardware for different use cases, mastering the intricacies of AI hardware is essential for anyone looking to delve into this rapidly evolving field.

One of the first considerations in designing AI hardware is the choice of neural network processor architecture. Different architectures, such as convolutional neural networks (CNNs) or recurrent neural networks (RNNs), have unique strengths and weaknesses that must be considered when selecting the best hardware for a particular task. Understanding these architectures and their requirements is crucial for building efficient and effective AI hardware solutions.

In addition to architecture considerations, it is also important to analyze the hardware requirements for training AI models. This includes factors such as computational power, memory bandwidth, and energy efficiency, all of which play a significant role in the performance of AI hardware. By understanding these requirements, developers can optimize their hardware design to meet the demands of training complex AI models.

Furthermore, optimizing AI hardware for specific use cases is essential for achieving optimal performance. Whether it be image recognition, natural language processing, or any other AI application, tailoring hardware design to the specific requirements of the task at hand can significantly improve efficiency and accuracy. This level of customization is key to unlocking the full potential of AI hardware in various real-world applications.

Overall, mastering the design and development of AI hardware requires a deep understanding of neural network processor components and functions, as well as a keen awareness of the latest advancements in AI hardware technology. By staying informed on the latest trends and techniques in AI hardware design, developers can build custom solutions that push the boundaries of what is possible in the world of artificial intelligence.

Chapter 9: Challenges and Limitations of Current AI Hardware

Power Consumption

In the realm of AI hardware, power consumption is a critical factor that must be carefully considered in the design and implementation of neural network processors. Power consumption refers to the amount of electrical energy consumed by a device or system during its operation, and it plays a significant role in determining the efficiency and performance of AI hardware.

When it comes to neural network processors, power consumption is particularly important due to the complex calculations and computations involved in training and running AI models. High power consumption can lead to increased heat generation, which can in turn affect the performance and longevity of the hardware. Therefore, optimizing power consumption is essential for ensuring the smooth and efficient operation of neural network processors.

There are several strategies that can be employed to minimize power consumption in AI hardware. One approach is to design energy-efficient architectures that prioritize performance while minimizing energy usage. This can involve using specialized hardware components, such as low-power processors and memory modules, that are specifically optimized for AI workloads.

Another way to reduce power consumption is through the implementation of advanced power management techniques, such as dynamic voltage and frequency scaling. These techniques allow the hardware to dynamically adjust its operating voltage and frequency based on the workload, thereby optimizing energy usage without sacrificing performance.

Overall, understanding and managing power consumption is crucial for maximizing the efficiency and effectiveness of AI hardware. By carefully considering power consumption in the design and implementation of neural network processors, developers can create hardware solutions that are not only powerful and capable, but also energy-efficient and sustainable in the long run.

Scalability Issues

Scalability is a critical issue in the world of AI hardware, as the demand for processing power continues to grow exponentially. For a person that wants to learn everything there is to know about AI hardware, understanding scalability issues is key to optimizing performance and efficiency. In this subchapter, we will delve into the challenges and solutions surrounding scalability in neural network processors and beyond.

One of the primary scalability issues in AI hardware is the ability to handle increasingly complex neural network models. As models become larger and more sophisticated, the hardware must be able to scale accordingly to support the growing computational requirements. This can be a significant challenge, as traditional hardware architectures may struggle to keep up with the demands of modern AI algorithms.

Another scalability issue to consider is the need for efficient parallel processing. Neural networks rely on parallel processing to accelerate training and inference tasks, but scaling up the number of processing units can introduce bottlenecks and inefficiencies. It is essential to design hardware with scalability in mind, ensuring that parallel processing can be effectively utilized without sacrificing performance.

Furthermore, the scalability of AI hardware is also influenced by the availability of memory and storage resources. As neural network models grow in size, the hardware must be able to accommodate the increasing data storage and memory requirements. This can be a limiting factor in the scalability of AI hardware, as inadequate memory or storage capacity can hinder the performance of neural network processors.

In conclusion, scalability is a crucial consideration in the design and implementation of AI hardware. For a person that wants to learn everything there is to know about AI hardware, understanding scalability issues is essential for optimizing performance and efficiency. By addressing challenges such as supporting complex models, efficient parallel processing, and adequate memory and storage resources, developers can build scalable AI hardware solutions that meet the growing demands of the industry.

Compatibility with Existing Systems

In the realm of artificial intelligence (AI), one of the key considerations for developers and engineers is ensuring compatibility with existing systems. This is particularly important when it comes to integrating new AI hardware, such as neural network processors, into established infrastructure. Understanding how these components interact with legacy systems is crucial for maximizing performance and efficiency.

When considering compatibility with existing systems, it is essential to take into account the architecture of the neural network processor. Different processors may have varying capabilities and specifications, which can impact how well they integrate with other hardware and software components. By conducting a detailed comparison of different neural network processor architectures, developers can identify the best fit for their specific needs and requirements.

Another important aspect to consider when integrating new AI hardware is the hardware requirements for training AI models. Training complex neural networks requires significant computational power and memory bandwidth, so it is essential to ensure that the existing system can support these demands. By analyzing the hardware requirements upfront, developers can avoid potential bottlenecks and ensure smooth operation of their AI models.

Optimizing AI hardware for specific use cases, such as image recognition or natural language processing, is another crucial consideration when it comes to compatibility with existing systems. By tailoring the hardware to the specific requirements of the application, developers can improve performance and efficiency. This may involve customizing the architecture of the neural network processor or fine-tuning parameters to better suit the workload.

Overall, ensuring compatibility with existing systems is a fundamental aspect of mastering AI hardware. By understanding the architecture of neural network processors, analyzing hardware requirements, optimizing for specific use cases, and considering the impact on the future of computing, developers can effectively integrate new AI hardware into their existing infrastructure. This comprehensive approach is essential for maximizing the potential of AI technology and driving innovation in the field.

Chapter 10: Comparison of Traditional Computer Hardware with Specialized AI Hardware

Performance Metrics

Performance metrics are essential when it comes to evaluating the efficiency and effectiveness of AI hardware. In this subchapter, we will delve into the various metrics that are used to measure the performance of neural network processors and other AI hardware components. These metrics include throughput, latency, power consumption, and accuracy, among others. By understanding these metrics, you will be able to make informed decisions when selecting AI hardware for your specific use case.

Throughput is a crucial performance metric that measures the number of operations that a neural network processor can perform in a given amount of time. A higher throughput indicates that the hardware can process more data in a shorter period, which is important for real-time applications such as autonomous vehicles or smart sensors. Latency, on the other hand, refers to the time it takes for a neural network processor to process a single input and produce an output. Low latency is critical for applications that require quick decision-making, such as facial recognition or fraud detection.

Power consumption is another important performance metric to consider when evaluating AI hardware. High power consumption can lead to increased operational costs and environmental impact, while low power consumption can result in longer battery life and reduced carbon footprint. Accuracy is perhaps the most crucial performance metric for AI applications, as it measures how well the hardware can perform a specific task compared to a human or benchmark standard. High accuracy is essential for applications such as medical diagnosis or financial forecasting, where precision is paramount.

In this subchapter, we will also explore how hardware requirements differ between training and inference stages of AI model development. Training a neural network requires more computational power and memory than inference, as it involves processing large datasets and optimizing model parameters. Understanding these hardware requirements is crucial for designing efficient AI hardware solutions that can meet the demands of your application. Additionally, we will discuss strategies for optimizing AI hardware for specific use cases, such as image recognition or natural language processing, to achieve the best performance and accuracy.

Overall, performance metrics play a vital role in the design, evaluation, and optimization of AI hardware. By mastering these metrics, you will be better equipped to select the right hardware for your specific application, whether it be for research or industry purposes. Stay tuned as we delve deeper into the latest advancements in AI hardware technology, the components and functions of neural network processors, and the impact of AI hardware on the future of computing.

Cost Analysis

Cost analysis is a crucial aspect to consider when delving into the realm of AI hardware. Understanding the expenses associated with neural network processors and other hardware components is essential for individuals looking to optimize their AI systems while staying within budget constraints. In this subchapter, we will explore the various factors that contribute to the overall cost of AI hardware, from the price of individual components to the expenses associated with training and maintenance.

One of the key considerations in cost analysis is the comparison of different neural network processor architectures. Each architecture comes with its own set of advantages and drawbacks, which can significantly impact the overall cost of the hardware. By conducting a detailed comparison of these architectures, individuals can make informed decisions on which type of processor best fits their needs and budget.

Another important aspect of cost analysis is understanding the hardware requirements for training AI models. Training AI models can be a resource-intensive process, requiring powerful hardware components such as GPUs and specialized processors. By analyzing the hardware requirements for training, individuals can better estimate the costs associated with building and maintaining their AI systems.

Optimizing AI hardware for specific use cases, such as image recognition or natural language processing, is also a key consideration in cost analysis. By tailoring the hardware to the specific needs of the application, individuals can maximize performance while minimizing costs. This customization allows for a more efficient use of resources and can ultimately lead to significant cost savings in the long run.

In conclusion, cost analysis is a critical component of mastering AI hardware. By carefully considering the expenses associated with neural network processors and other hardware components, individuals can make informed decisions on how to optimize their AI systems while staying within budget constraints. By comparing different architectures, analyzing hardware requirements, and optimizing for specific use cases, individuals can build cost-effective AI solutions that meet their needs and deliver optimal performance.

Future Trends

In the rapidly evolving field of artificial intelligence, staying ahead of future trends in AI hardware is crucial for anyone looking to maximize the potential of neural network processors and other cutting-edge technologies. As new advancements continue to shape the landscape of AI hardware, it is important to understand the key trends that will drive innovation in the coming years.

One of the most significant future trends in AI hardware is the development of more specialized neural network processor architectures. These architectures are designed to optimize performance for specific tasks, such as image recognition or natural language processing, by leveraging the unique characteristics of neural networks. By tailoring hardware to meet the demands of specific AI applications, researchers and developers can achieve higher levels of efficiency and accuracy in their models.

Another key trend to watch for in the world of AI hardware is the increasing focus on optimizing hardware for energy efficiency. As AI models grow larger and more complex, the amount of computational power required to train these models continues to rise. By developing hardware solutions that are more energy-efficient, researchers can reduce the environmental impact of AI technology while also lowering the cost of training and deploying AI models.

In addition to advancements in specialized architectures and energy efficiency, future trends in AI hardware will also include a greater emphasis on custom solutions for specific use cases. Whether researchers are looking to build custom hardware for research purposes or industry applications, the ability to tailor hardware to meet the unique demands of a given task will be crucial for driving innovation in the field of artificial intelligence.

Overall, the future of AI hardware promises to be an exciting and dynamic landscape, with new advancements and trends shaping the way we approach neural network processing and other AI technologies. By staying informed on the latest developments in AI hardware and understanding how these trends will impact the future of computing, researchers and developers can position themselves for success in this rapidly evolving field.

Chapter 11: Environmental Impact and Sustainability Measures

Energy Efficiency

Energy efficiency is a crucial aspect of AI hardware design, as it directly impacts the performance and power consumption of neural network processors. In this subchapter, we will delve into the importance of energy efficiency in AI hardware and explore various techniques to optimize energy consumption.

One of the key considerations in designing energy-efficient AI hardware is minimizing power consumption without compromising performance. This can be achieved through various methods, such as optimizing the architecture of neural network processors, implementing efficient algorithms, and utilizing low-power components.

Furthermore, energy efficiency in AI hardware is not just about reducing power consumption during operation, but also during the training phase. Training AI models requires significant computational resources, which can lead to high energy consumption. By optimizing hardware for training tasks, such as utilizing parallel processing units and efficient memory systems, energy consumption can be significantly reduced.

In addition to optimizing energy efficiency in AI hardware, it is important to consider the environmental impact of these technologies. As the demand for AI hardware continues to grow, so does the energy consumption and carbon footprint associated with these devices. Therefore, sustainability measures, such as using renewable energy sources and designing recyclable hardware components, are essential for mitigating the environmental impact of AI hardware.

Overall, energy efficiency plays a crucial role in the design and development of AI hardware, as it not only impacts performance and power consumption but also influences the environmental sustainability of these technologies. By implementing energy-efficient design strategies and considering the environmental impact of AI hardware, we can ensure a more sustainable future for AI computing.

E-waste Management

In the realm of artificial intelligence technology, the management of electronic waste, or e-waste, has become a crucial aspect to consider. As the demand for AI hardware like neural network processors continues to grow, it is essential to address the environmental impact of disposing of outdated or obsolete equipment. E-waste management involves the proper disposal, recycling, and reuse of electronic devices to minimize the negative effects on the environment and human health.

One of the key considerations in e-waste management is the recycling and refurbishment of AI hardware components. Neural network processors, for example, contain valuable materials such as semiconductors and rare earth elements that can be salvaged and reused in new devices. By implementing efficient recycling processes, we can reduce the need for raw materials extraction and minimize the environmental footprint of AI hardware production.

Furthermore, e-waste management also involves the responsible disposal of electronic devices that have reached the end of their useful life. Improper disposal of AI hardware can lead to toxic substances leaching into the soil and water, posing risks to ecosystems and human populations. It is essential for individuals and organizations to follow proper disposal guidelines and work with certified e-waste recycling facilities to ensure that electronic devices are recycled or disposed of safely.

In addition to recycling and disposal, another important aspect of e-waste management is the design of AI hardware with sustainability in mind. Manufacturers can incorporate eco-friendly materials, energy-efficient components, and modular designs that facilitate easy repair and upgrade. By prioritizing sustainability in the design and production of AI hardware, we can minimize the environmental impact of electronic waste and contribute to a more sustainable future.

Overall, e-waste management is a critical consideration in the development and use of AI hardware like neural network processors. By implementing efficient recycling processes, responsible disposal practices, and sustainable design strategies, we can reduce the environmental impact of electronic waste and promote a more sustainable approach to artificial intelligence technology.

Green Computing Initiatives

Green computing initiatives are becoming increasingly important in the world of AI hardware. As technology continues to advance at a rapid pace, the demand for more powerful and energy-efficient hardware solutions is on the rise. In this subchapter, we will explore some of the key initiatives that are being implemented to reduce the environmental impact of AI hardware and promote sustainability in the industry.

One of the most significant green computing initiatives in AI hardware is the development of energy-efficient neural network processors. These specialized processors are designed to optimize power consumption while still delivering high performance for tasks such as training and inference. By reducing the energy requirements of these processors, companies can lower their carbon footprint and contribute to a more sustainable future.

Another important aspect of green computing initiatives in AI hardware is the use of renewable energy sources to power data centers and other computing facilities. By harnessing the power of solar, wind, or other sustainable energy sources, companies can reduce their dependence on fossil fuels and minimize their impact on the environment. This approach not only helps to reduce greenhouse gas emissions but also lowers operating costs for businesses in the long run.

In addition to energy efficiency and renewable energy sources, green computing initiatives in AI hardware also focus on reducing electronic waste and promoting recycling. As technology continues to evolve, older hardware components are often discarded in favor of newer, more advanced models. By implementing recycling programs and encouraging the reuse of components, companies can minimize the environmental impact of their hardware and contribute to a more circular economy.

Overall, green computing initiatives play a crucial role in shaping the future of AI hardware. By prioritizing energy efficiency, renewable energy sources, and recycling practices, companies can help to mitigate the environmental impact of their hardware and pave the way for a more sustainable and eco-friendly industry. As we continue to push the boundaries of AI technology, it is essential that we also consider the environmental consequences of our actions and work towards a more sustainable future for all.

Conclusion: The Future of AI Hardware

In conclusion, the future of AI hardware is incredibly promising, with advancements being made at a rapid pace. As we continue to push the boundaries of technology, we can expect to see neural network processors and other specialized hardware becoming more powerful and efficient. This will enable us to train AI models faster and more accurately, ultimately leading to groundbreaking discoveries and applications in various fields.

One of the key takeaways from this comprehensive guide is the importance of understanding the different neural network processor architectures available. By being knowledgeable about the various options and their capabilities, individuals can make informed decisions when choosing hardware for their AI projects. This can result in significant improvements in performance and efficiency, ultimately leading to better outcomes and results.

Furthermore, optimizing AI hardware for specific use cases, such as image recognition or natural language processing, is crucial for achieving optimal performance. By tailoring hardware configurations to meet the unique requirements of each application, individuals can maximize the efficiency of their AI systems and achieve superior results. This level of customization is essential for pushing the boundaries of what is possible with AI technology.

As we look towards the future, it is clear that AI hardware will play a central role in shaping the future of computing. With the latest advancements in technology, we can expect to see even more powerful and efficient hardware solutions being developed. This will open up new possibilities for research and industry applications, paving the way for groundbreaking discoveries and innovations in the field of artificial intelligence.

Despite the challenges and limitations that currently exist in AI hardware, the potential for growth and advancement is immense. By continuing to push the boundaries of technology and explore new possibilities, we can expect to see significant improvements in the performance and efficiency of AI hardware. This will ultimately lead to a future where AI systems are more capable, versatile, and impactful than ever before.

www.ingramcontent.com/pod-product-compliance
Lightning Source LLC
LaVergne TN
LVHW081807050326
832903LV00027B/2138